The Ballet of Violence

Photography by
Monte Gerlach

Ballet of Violence

Face Time Books
504 Forest Preserve Dr.
La Grange Park, IL 60526
708-354-3255
gerlach@sxu.edu

Library of Congress Control Number: 2010942647

Gerlach, Monte
    Ballet of Violence
        Photographs by Monte Gerlach - 1st edition
    ISBN 978-0-615-42665-5
    1. Photography - Professional Wrestling, sport, art, etc.

Copyright © 2010 by Monte H. Gerlach

All rights reserved.
Except as permitted under the U.S. Copyright Act of 1976, no part of this publication may be reproduced, distributed, or transmitted in any form or by any means, or stored in a database retrieval system, without the prior written permission of the author.

Cover Design by Megan Kowalski

Acknowledgements

I would like to express my deepest gratitude to Nicole Gerlach and Jeannie Hallaren for their editing and proofreading skills. Megan Kowalski's cover design and continued technical support were invaluable in the completion of this book.
M. H. G.

ISBN 978-0-615-42665-5

Introduction

Thursday night in America's heartland, All Star Wrestling was on the air. As an eight-year-old boy, I was glued to our black-and-white small screen television as the local station broadcast live professional wrestling. Those big men in their bathing suits tossing one another around the ring fascinated me, and on occasion terrified me as well.

One wrestler in particular caused childhood nightmares: "The Wild Bull of the Pampas," Pampero Firpo. He had long black hair down to his shoulders, a full beard, and bear-like hair all over his body, unlike most of his shorthaired, clean-shaven opponents whom he always dominated. He was a "heel," a villain, a part that he played to perfection in my terrified eight-year-old imagination. Pampero Firpo carried a shrunken head, and his guttural English came out a deep resonant growl. He would rumble into the camera "OOOH YEEAAH" and then proceed to take apart his luckless victim for that match. He was the scariest figure in my world but I couldn't stop watching him. He was real, he was dangerous, and he was in my small town.

At that time my mother worked as a waitress in the Silver Grill Cafe. When Pampero was in town for a match, he would eat at the cafe, and my mother got to know him. When she told him how much he frightened her young son, he gave her a publicity photo for me, and later I got the chance to meet him. In person he was still rather different-looking from anyone I'd ever seen, but he wasn't as scary as I had imagined him.

Pampero Firpo's real name was Juan Kachmanian. A native of Argentina, he took his ring name and his nickname from the famous Argentine boxer Luis Angel Firpo, who called himself "Pampero, the Wild Bull of the Pampas." Kachmanian was a hardcore wrestler, which means that he did not follow match rules and favored foreign objects. He wrestled as a heel for most of his career. That was until The Sheik fireballed him, launching Kachmanian's brief stint as a "baby face," or good guy. He held a number of titles in the USA and South America. His signature moves were the El Grafio and the bear hug. He retired in 1986, and then went to work for the United States Postal Service in San Jose, California.

I never got to photograph the Wild Bull, but he represented an important lesson as I thought about photographing wrestling. On Thursday Night All Star Wrestling he was the epitome of evil, a truly terrifying figure, but when I met him he was polite, kind, and soft-spoken. The dichotomy of his image as a wrestler and the man I met eating pot roast called into question the truth of All Star Wrestling. On live television wrestling looked so real. The drama was so emotional, the heels were so bad, and the baby faces were so likeable. To my eight-year-old brain it summed up the titanic struggles of life, or at least what I thought that the titanic struggles of life should be. I was so emotionally invested in the drama as it played out in 15 minute falls on Thursday night that it had to be real.

I inevitably grew up, and yes, I finally stopped believing in Santa Claus and in Professional Wrestling. However, when I started photographing wrestling, the fictional nature of professional wrestling wasn't important. The fact that wrestling was choreographed and loosely scripted was the very thing that attracted me to it. I found the way wrestling represented real fights very close to how photography represented reality; photos too are loosely scripted and often choreographed. I always begin the first day of photography class with "Monte's Laws of Photography." My number one "law" is that "All Photographs Lie" - and the next logical corollary of that axiom is "therefore all photographers are liars."

Photographs lie and those who make them are liars: a good way to start a book on wrestling. Photographs lie because photographers have so much control; they pick the angle, the lens, the exposure, often the lighting, and the moment that the shutter is released. All of this control occurs before the image is captured; we all know what can be done to a picture once it is in a computer, in postproduction. But the most important reason that photographs are not the truth is that people believe that they are, much like wrestling fans who let themselves believe that what they are witnessing in the ring is real violence and mayhem. Both audiences accept that what they see is real and an accurate depiction of the world, when is just an illusion.

Garry Winogrand was fond of saying, "I photograph to see how things look photographed." This project is not a documentary on boxing or wrestling. I am not out to do an exposé on the theatricality of wrestling. On the contrary, it is that very theatricality that drew me to pick wrestling as a subject in the first place. I started this series with boxing: two guys in a small ring trying to punch each other's lights out. Boxing, for the most part, is neither scripted nor choreographed. My original idea was to use the action in boxing to explore figures in motion. However, I found that boxing, for all its gritty reality, was visually repetitive. One bout photographed like the next. There was drama, action, winners and losers, but each fight was the same dance, using the same motions.

Wrestling is never the same visually. The combatants are characters in the classic struggle of good vs. evil. If two wrestlers have the same sort of reputation, or even if the fans do not know anything about them, within minutes of the beginning of a match everyone knows who is the face and who is the heel. I have photographed the same wrestlers at different venues. While they were usually consistent - the baby faces stayed good and the heels stayed bad - occasionally two heels or two faces were matched together, and the crowd always picked one to cheer for. In professional wrestling the script of each bout is basically the same, and the wrestlers have their signature moves, holds, and general shtick. Yet each match had enough variations that they always produced fresh images.

Many people dismiss wrestling as faked violence for the masses. When I was a newspaper photographer the local wrestling promoter came to see the sports editor. He wanted to have his events covered by the local paper. The editor, trying to find a polite way of saying no, told him that the matches ended too late, way after the paper's production deadline.

The guy replied, "I will give you the results before the matches." We were never allowed to shoot professional wrestling for the newspaper.

When you are leaning under the bottom rope and a 280 pound man is being tossed around the ring in front of you, it is hard to believe that it is an illusion. The men and women of professional wrestling are very good athletes. Their bodies take an enormous amount of abuse, faked or not. They can improvise, react, and stay in character, selling the brutality, the drama, and the pain of their sport. Often times I would hear them growling to each other about what was to happen next. On one memorable occasion a wrestler said to me, "You had better move your ass, kid, because he's coming over the top rope right here." I did not have to be told twice, and as I quickly moved to the side his opponent sailed out of the ring and landed right where I had been standing.

This project came about by my searching for the unnoticed, the invisible, and the overlooked. At the Institute of Design at IIT, I was confronted with the fact that almost everything has been photographed before. Graduate students were told that if you wanted to be original you had to find a totally new subject or photograph the world in a new way. I have always been interested in how motion is captured by film. For my graduate thesis I built a slit camera to photograph motion in a new way. A slit camera is what is used at the finish line in horse racing to record the photo-finish. Motorized film is pulled past a slit, which is lined up on the finish line. A photo-finish is not an instant in time. It is an extended moment as the film moves at the same speed as the running horses, and records not only which horse's nose crosses the line first, but also the position of all of the horses over time, as they crossed over the finish line and thus in front of the slit in the camera. For my thesis, I used nudes moving in a studio, and the effects that the moving film and narrow slit created resulted in images of figures in space that were completely different from what the eye sees. I have also used infrared film to see how it captures motion with light that is invisible to the human eye. The exploration of movement of figures through time and space was a general theme in my early work.

Shutter drag is one of the photographic terms used to describe the technique that I employed on these images. It is basically a double exposure: one exposure from a flash, and the other from a long shutter (drag) exposure. The flash freezes the action, creating that instant in time; the long open shutter blurs the action, creating a virtual volume of the figure's movement over space and time. This is neither the "truth" nor reality as we can perceive it; our eyes cannot stop motion nor can we see movement over time. Our threshold of discernment is about 1/30 of a second. Anything faster than that is a blur or disappears completely. Our brain can chart a figure's movement as it passes through time and space, but it does not record motion as a continuous track – unless it is very bright, like 4th of July sparklers that burn an afterimage on our rods and cones. I had used this shutter drag technique in my street photography, portraiture, and in photographing dance. When I applied it to professional wrestling, a much-photographed cultural phenomenon, I knew I had something fresh.

In 1937, Alexey Brodovitch, the legendary art director of Harper's Bazaar, photographed ballet with a slow shutter. His blurred images were a revolution in how dance could be depicted. Lois Greenfield in the 1980s used studio strobes and a dance troupe that would repeat leaps over and over until she captured those incredible frozen moments of floating dancers. Dance has been photographed by a number of talented and visionary photographers over the last century.

With shutter drag I found a technique that recorded both the frozen instant and the extended blur of motion, giving me a different way of seeing action. However, I found it difficult to photograph dance in live performances due to restricted access, so I went searching for other public displays of motion and emotion. I tried boxing first, then I remembered my childhood fascination with wrestling. Using the strobe to stop motion and the long open shutter to blur the motion created the perfect tension between the frozen expression of the wrestler's face and the path of their trajectory. From the first time I photographed a wrestling match, I knew I had a project that should be explored. Whenever I could get away from my teaching responsibilities, I would go photograph a wrestling match.

Wrestling has been the subject of art throughout recorded history. One wrestling historian claimed that wrestling images can be traced back 15,000 years to cave drawings in France. I cannot verify that claim, but certainly early Egyptian and Babylonian reliefs depict wrestlers using holds of the present day sport. In ancient Greece, wrestling occupied a prominent place in legends and literature. Wrestling was the featured sport in early Olympic games. The Romans borrowed it from the Greeks. During the Middle Ages wrestlers had the patronage of many royal families.

English colonists brought the tradition to the New World and found that wrestling was already practiced among Native American peoples. Amateur wrestling thrived throughout the early years of the nation, and served as a popular activity at county fairs and celebrations. Modern-day professional wrestling grew out of the traveling carnival tradition of the strong man taking on all comers to stay in the ring with him for a set amount of time.

Thomas Eakins, American realist painter and photographer, used wrestling as a subject. Photographer, Eadweard Muybridge made wrestler's movements a series of plates in his important book Human and Animal Locomotion. Francis Bacon's painting "Some Phases in a Wrestling Match" was inspired by Muybridge's frames and portrayed the action and drama of the physical contest. Picasso also created several drawings of wrestling matches. Wrestling is a natural subject for art because of its intense focus on the human struggle.

In life as well as photography, timing is everything. In the late 1970s and early 1980s, professional wrestling was still a regional affair. Each region had its own stable of wrestlers and its own champions. The matches were held in small auditoriums, school gyms, and VFW halls. Poughkeepsie, NY was the largest town in which I photographed wrestling. Yes, Madison Square Garden was hosting the title bouts, but I never tried to photograph there. I loved the small, dimly lit arenas. With two Nikon cameras slung around me, I was always let in for free and allowed to lean into the ring under the ropes. There were rarely barricades to keep the fans out, but I was usually the only photographer shooting. I would have never have been allowed such intimate access in the big venues. Small towns filled with enthusiastic fans were what I needed. The wrestlers always put on a good show and the fans were always interesting.

At first I ignored the fans. They were behind me and not important to the action happening in the ring. Then I began to notice how involved they were in the action. These were not passive spectators at normal sporting events; these were Romans at the Coliseum watching gladiators. Sports fans generally cheer or boo during the course of the game, such as when there is a great play or a tragic mistake is made. Most of the time the audience is just silent. Wrestling fans start cheering or booing when the combatants are introduced, and continue vocalizing until the last man stumbles out of the ring at the end of the night. Choreography has to have music, and it seems to me that the fans provided the accompaniment to the brutal spectacle. The wrestlers seemed to tune into their vocalizations, and would typically play to the crowd.

Professional wrestling was undergoing a major upheaval in the late 1970s and early 1980s. The Northeast region of the National Wrestling Alliance (NWA) was under the control of Vince J. McMahon. McMahon broke away from NWA after Andre the Giant became the company's top star, and formed the World Wide Wrestling Federation (WWWF) in 1973. McMahon eventually sold his company to his son Vince K. McMahon Jr. The young McMahon grew the fan base through the use of marketing and television. He recruited Hulk Hogan, who had appeared in Rocky III and had a cartoon show. In 1985, he promoted Wrestlemania at Madison Square Garden and used pay-per-view and closed circuit TV throughout the country. The age of the wrestling soap opera and superstar wrestling actors was born, and the small town venues were drying up.

Time has a way of changing what you intended to do and what you end up with. In 1984, I showed this work to a friend and fellow photographer, who told me it was too journalistic. I had recently changed jobs from teaching in a School of Journalism to teaching in an Art department. "Being too journalistic" wasn't what I wanted to hear. I was not doing a documentary project; as far as I was concerned, I was trying to make art. I often did not record the names of the wrestlers in the bouts or who won, since that wasn't important to the pictures or the project. It was their motion and emotions that I was interested in. My friend's "journalistic" comment and the fact that wrestling was changing, growing out of its regional small town roots to become the giant entertainment industry that it is today, caused me to put the photos in a file cabinet and pursue other projects.

Twenty five years later, I received a year-long sabbatical from teaching to organize and publish my early work. When I came across the wrestling photos, they still seemed fresh and interesting, even after all this time. The series is not a complete document of wrestling in the early 1980s, but all photographs are documents of some sort. The years since these photos were taken have given them a historical significance. They show famous wrestlers like Hulk Hogan, who was just getting started as a heel, and Andre the Giant, who was just winding down his stellar career. Many of the wrestlers in my photographs I cannot identify. These guys were known as the "prelim" or "jobber" wrestlers. They would wrestle a big-name wrestler, always taking enormous punishment and losing to him. I cannot find out who they were, but they made great subjects for my photographs.

Perhaps artistic wrestling photos are not what the hard-core wrestling fan wants to see. Looking at professional wrestling photographs of the last 30 years, the façade of the phony becomes so apparent. Even the action shots look staged. Combining a moving wrestler that is frozen with the trail that his movement carves through space-time gives me a unique way of photographing wrestling. Where the movement, the emotions, and the brutality, all combine into a dance: a ballet of violence.

Monte Gerlach

Golden Gloves

Chicago, 1978

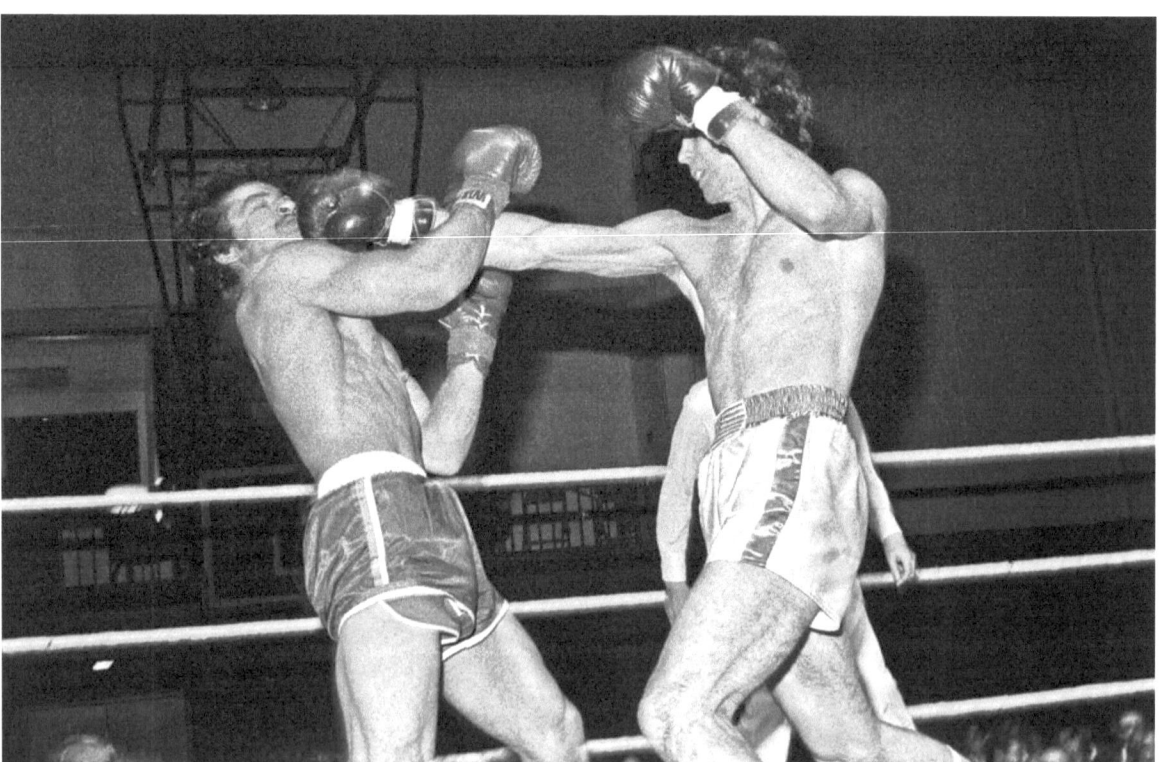

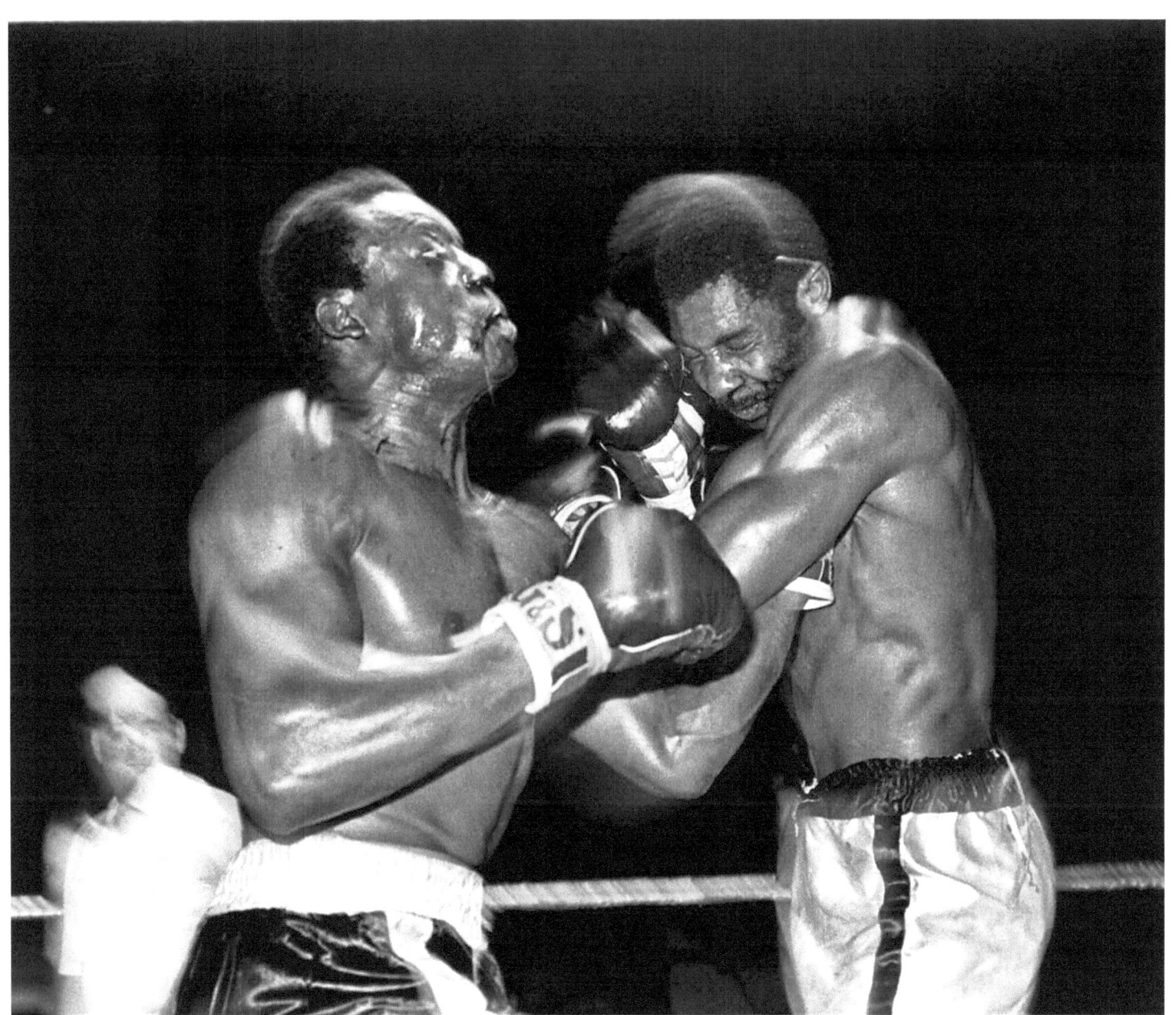

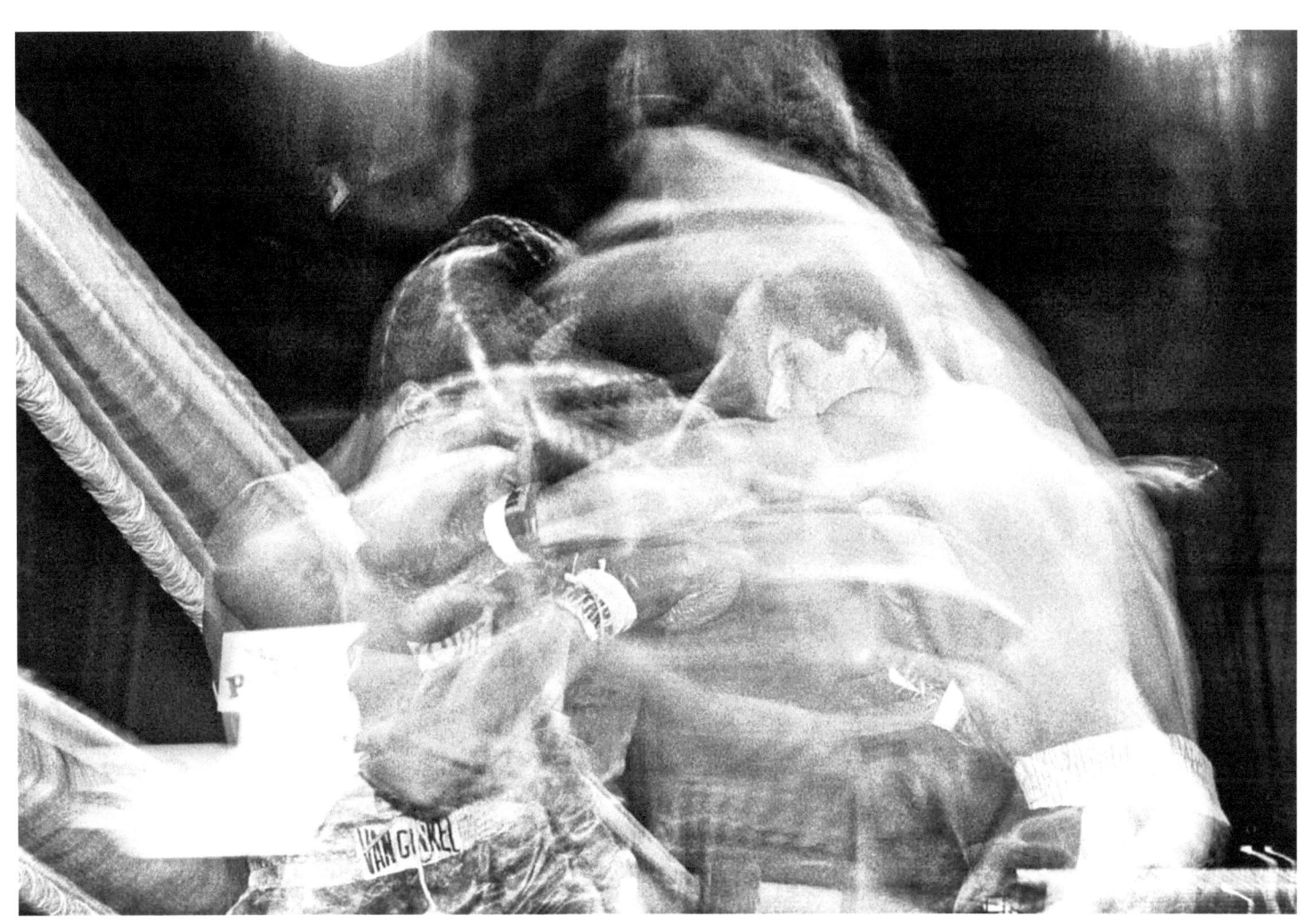

World Wrestling Federation

Small Towns in
New York and New Jersey
1979-1984

The Crusher vs. Bobby Duncum, 1979

Pat Paterson vs. Chief Jules Strongbow (Frank Hill) 1979

Ivan Koloff, 1979

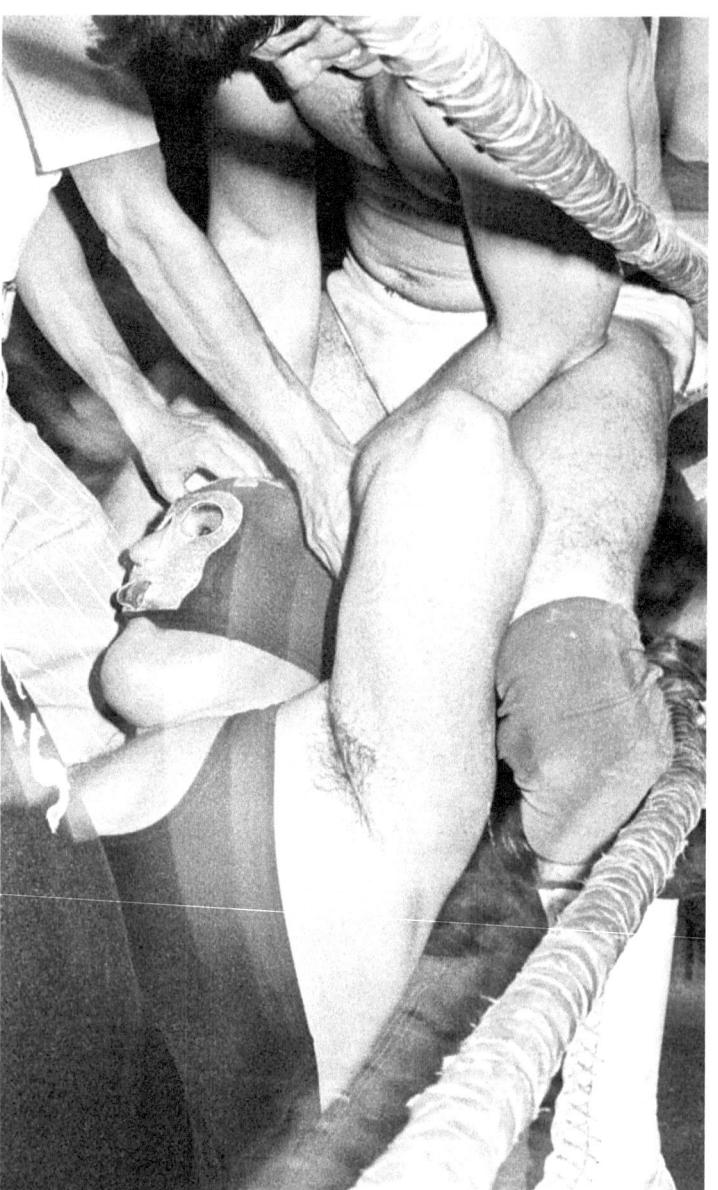

Super D, 1979

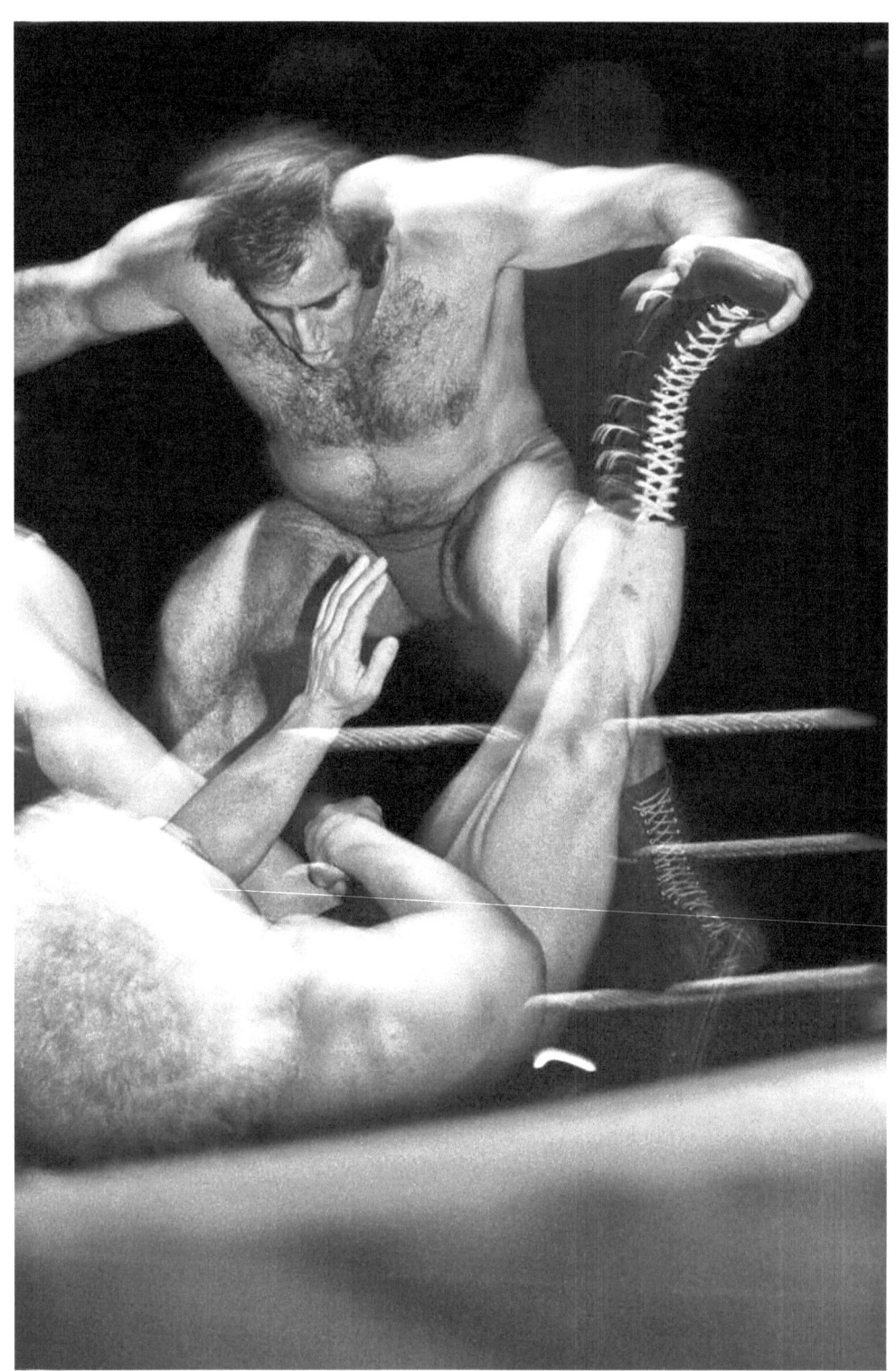

Baron Mikel Scicluna
vs. Ken Patera, 1980

Johnny Rodz vs. Angelo Gomez, 1980

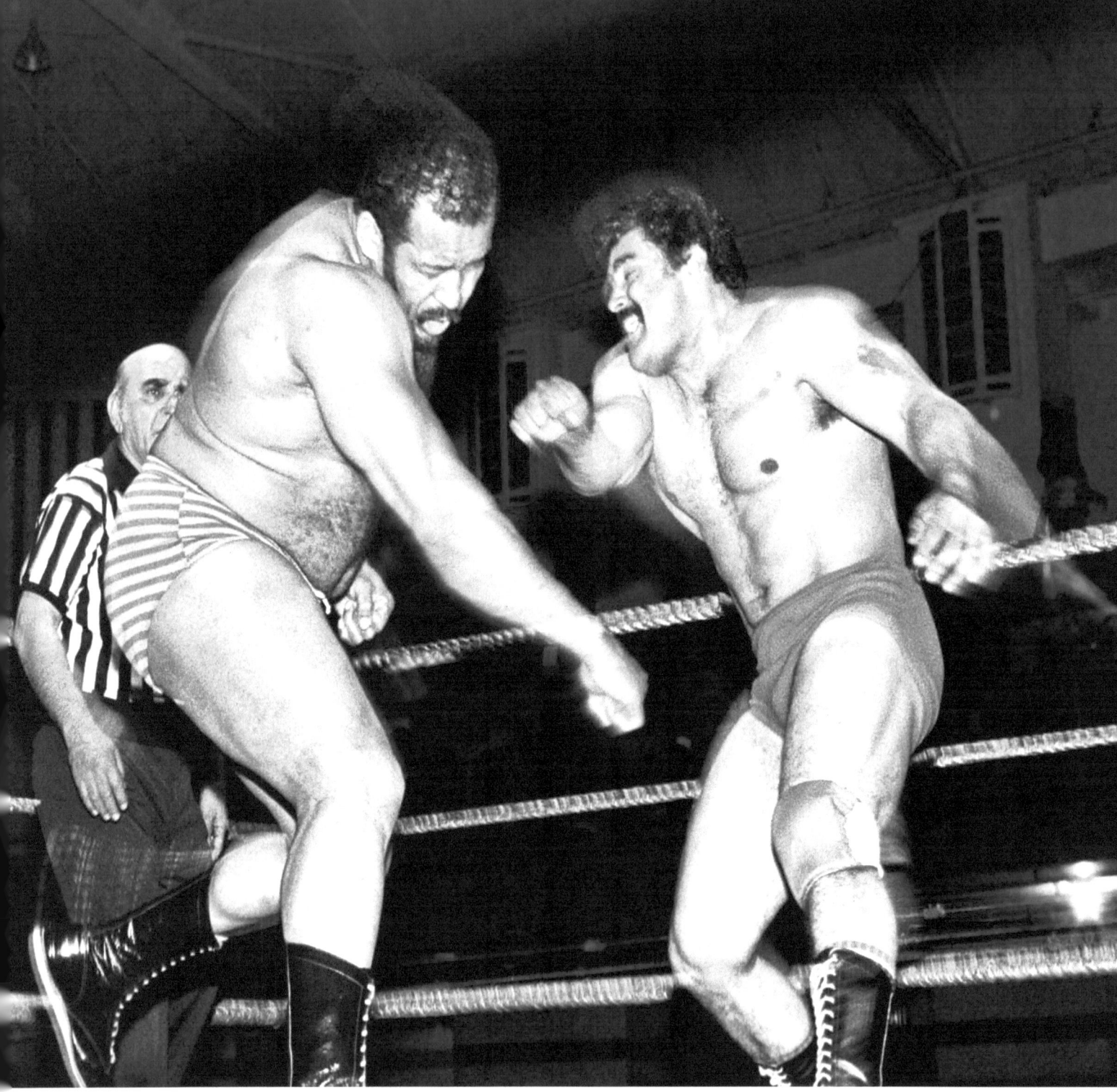

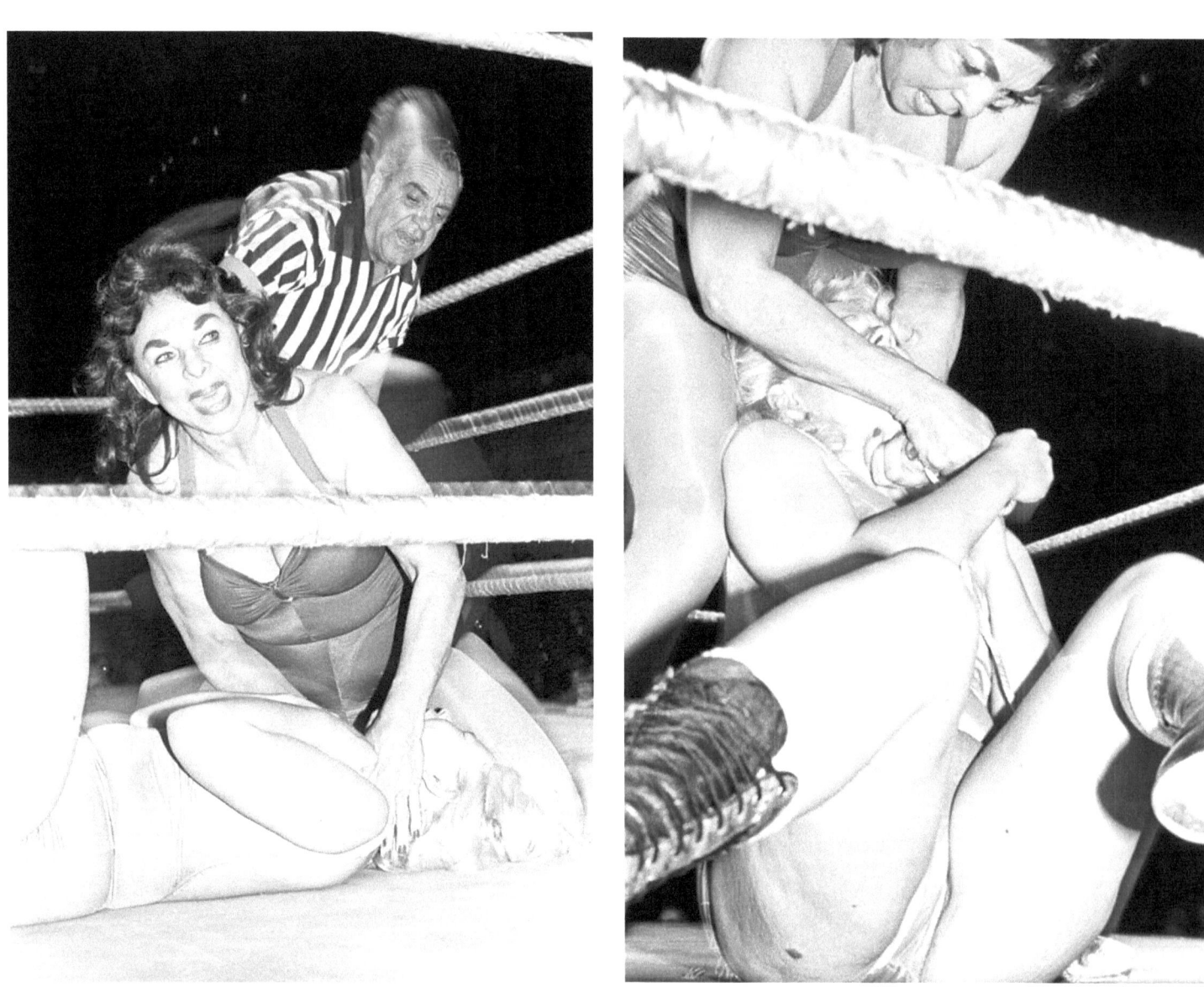

Fabulous Moolah in a tag team match, 1980

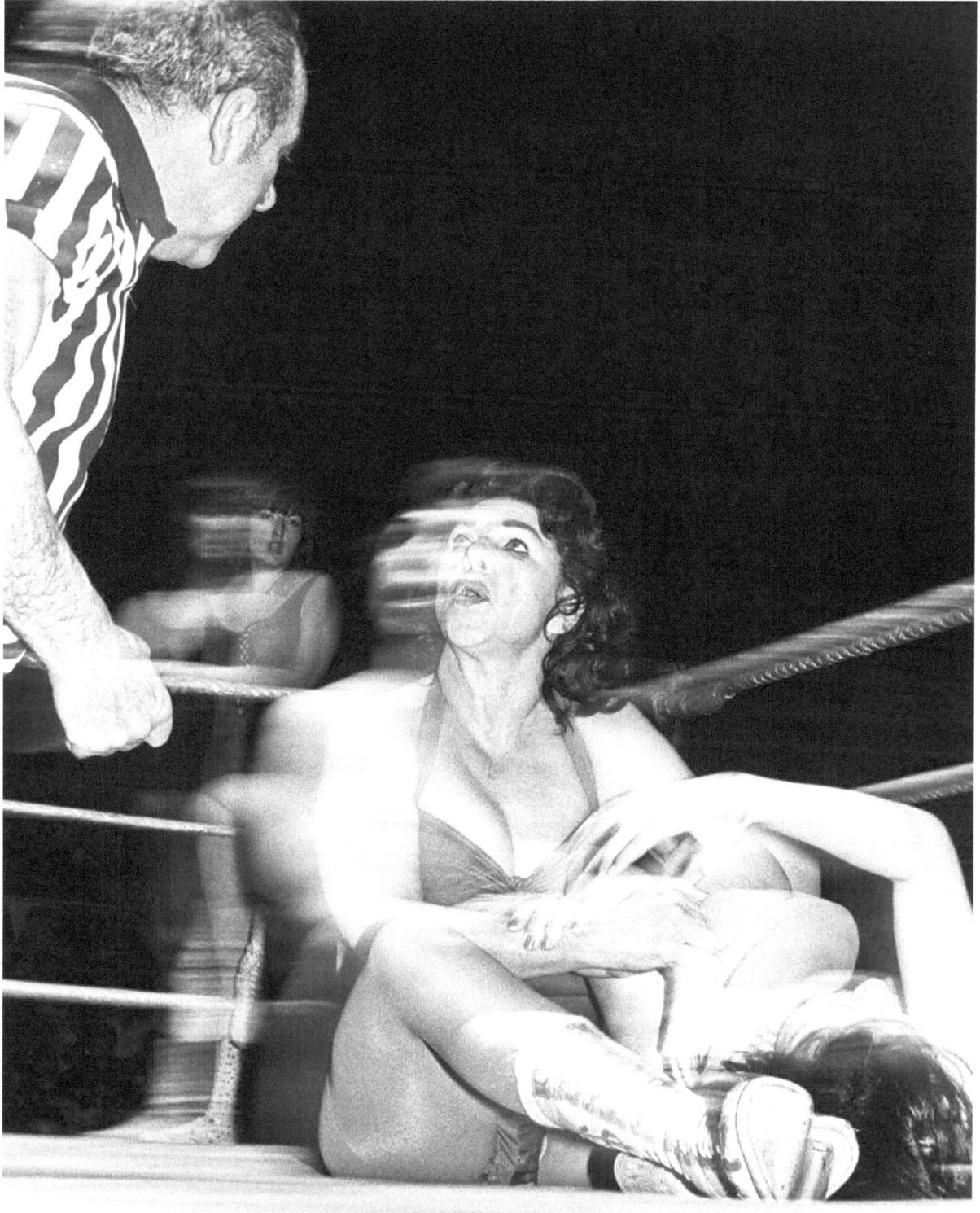

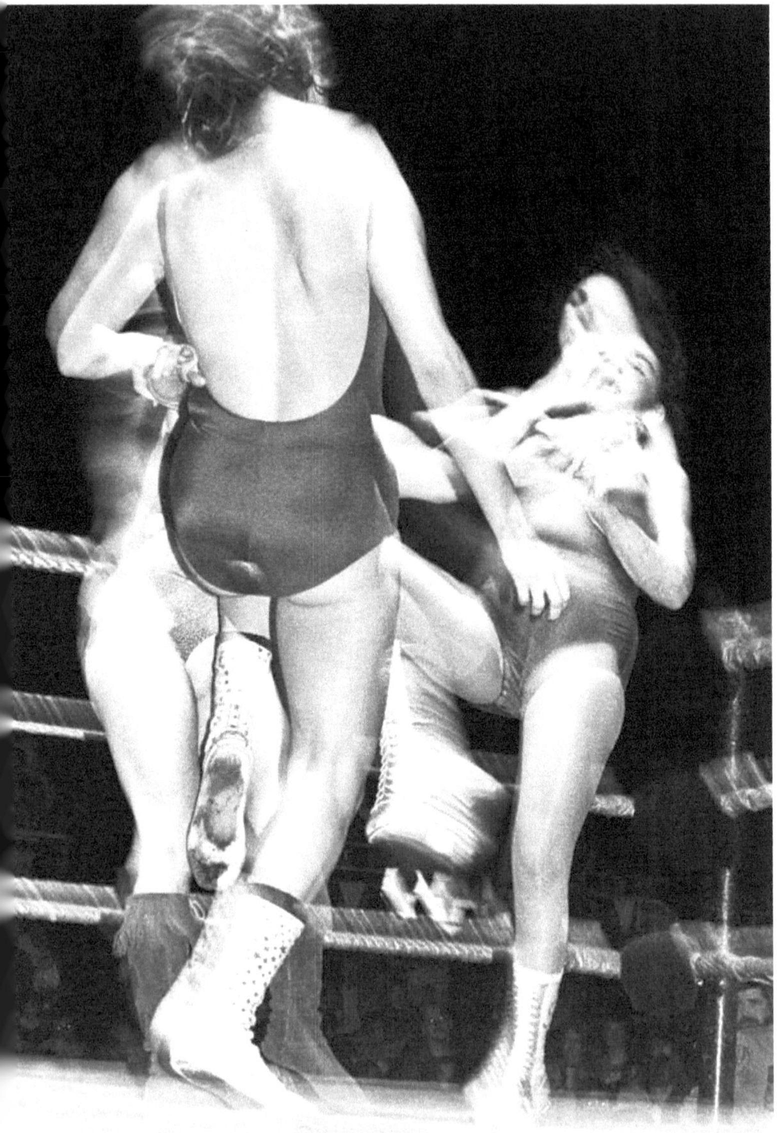

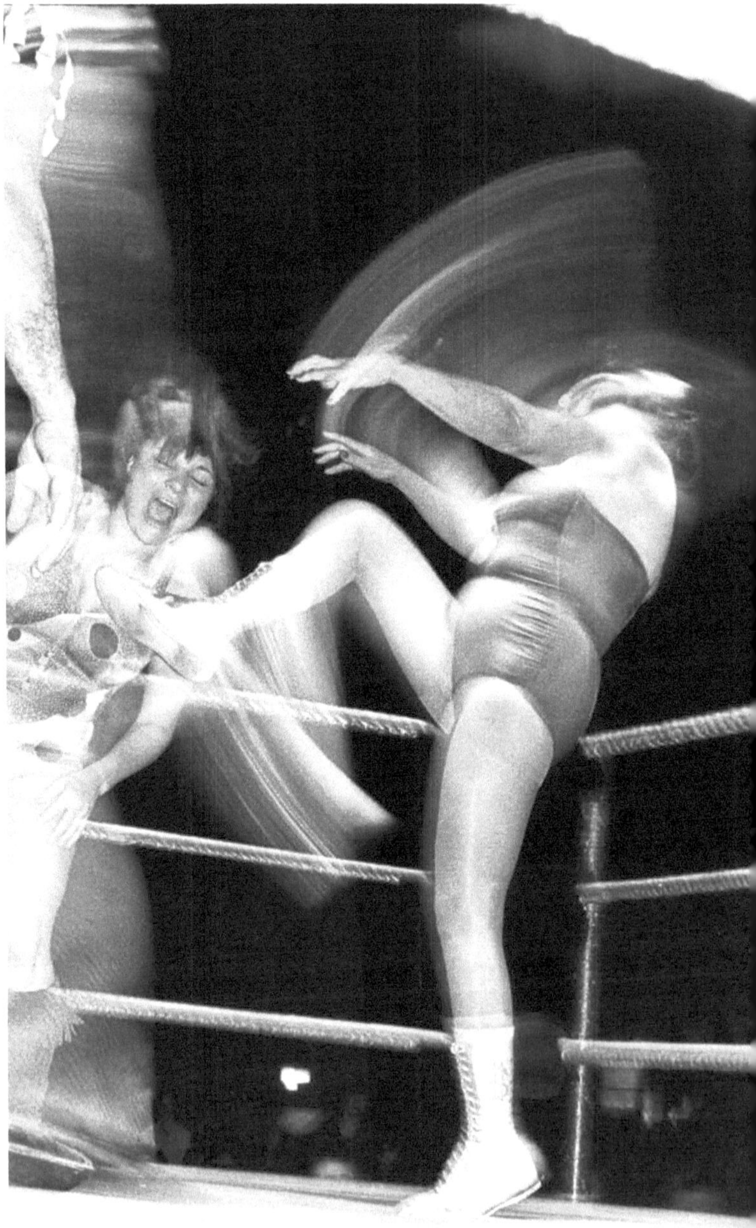

Rene Goulet vs. Larry Zbyszko, 1980

Pat Patterson vs. Captain Lou Albano, 1980

Tito Santana, holder of the championship title, 1980

Ivan Putski, "Polish Power" vs. Bobby Duncum, 1980

Davey O'Hanan, 1980

Baron Mikel Scicluna vs. Davey O'Hanan, 1980

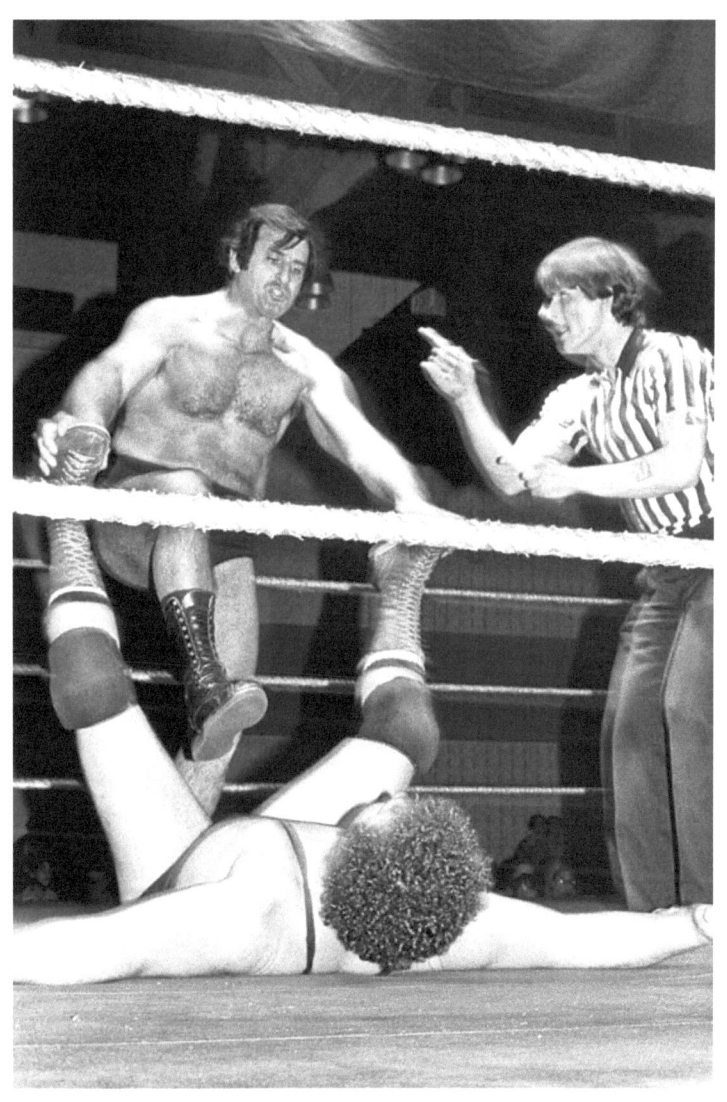 

Larry Zabisko vs. Frank Williams, 1980

Wild Samoans, Afa and Sika, 1980

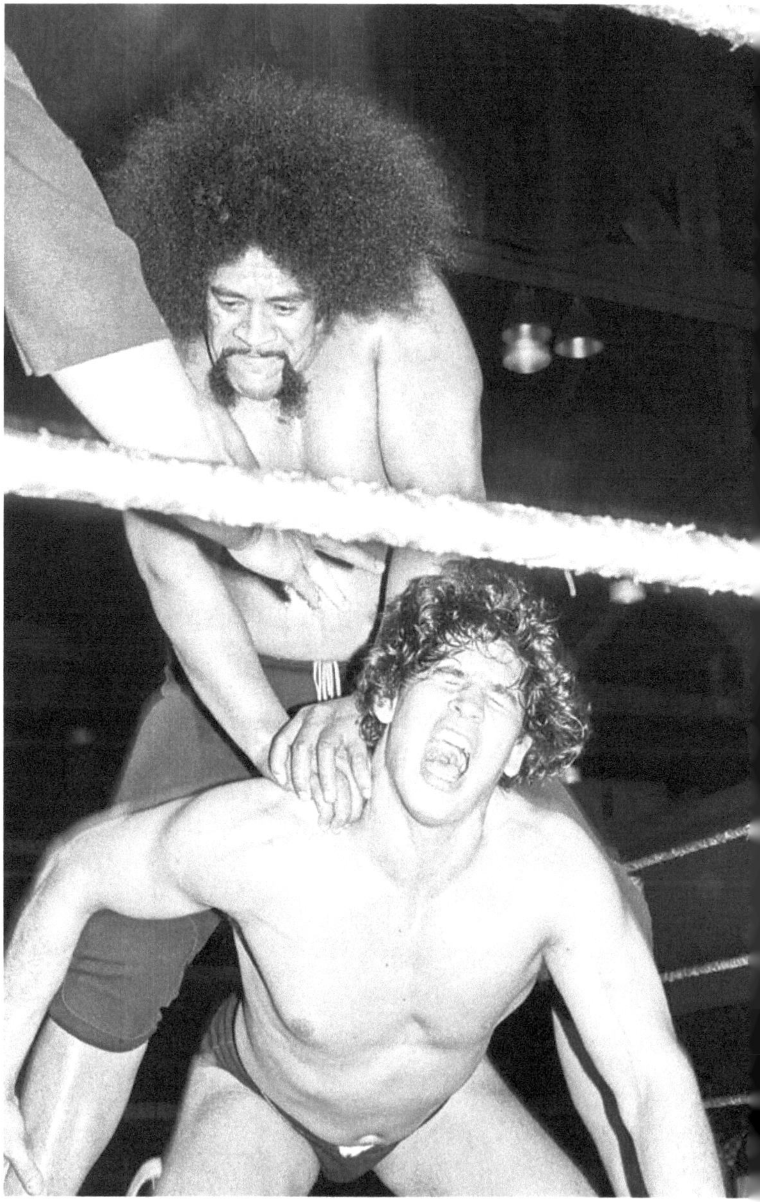

Wild Samoans vs. Tito Santana and Ivan Putski in a tag team match, 1980

Ivan Putski and Tito Santana slam the Wild Somoans together as their manager Bobby Heenan protests, 1980.

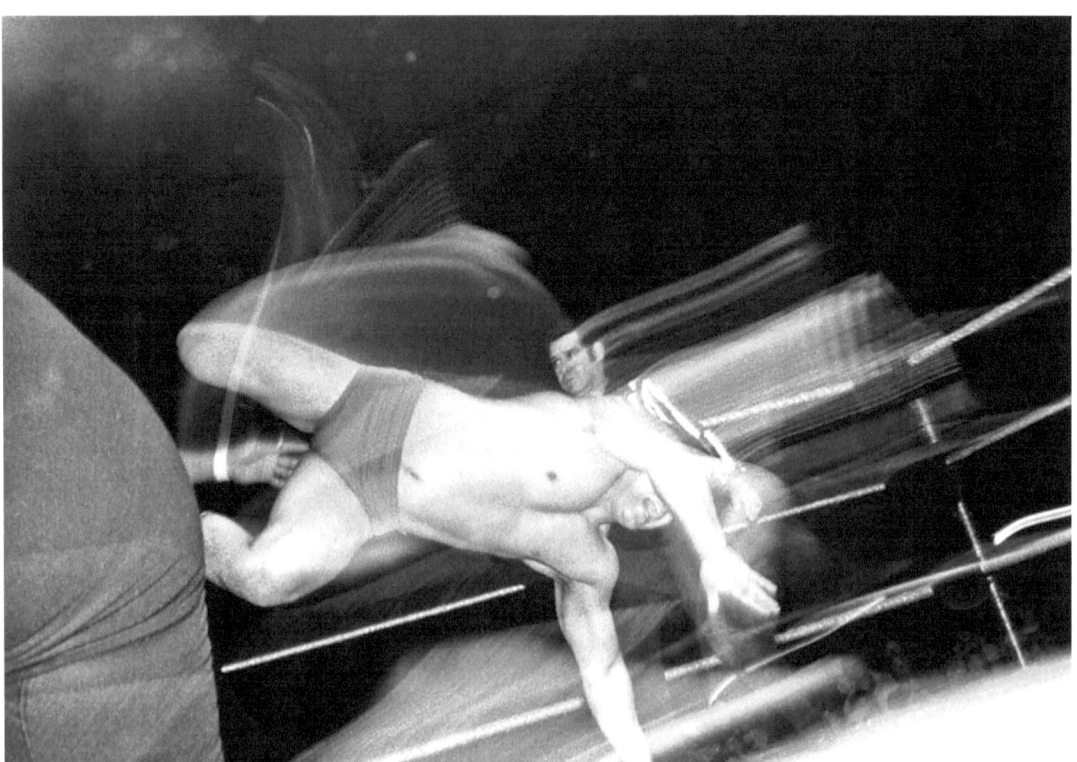

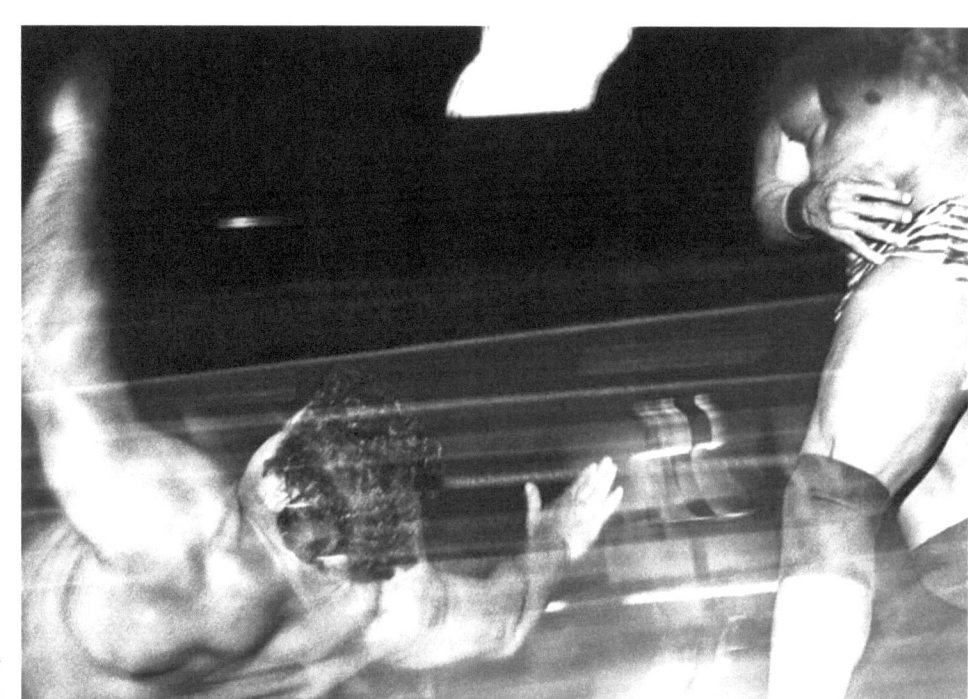

Jimmy "Superfly" Snuka
vs. Pedro Morales, 1982

Pedro Morales, 1982

Chief Jules Strongbow (Frank Hill), 1982

Chief Jules Strongbow (Frank Hill) vs. Mr. Fiji, 1982

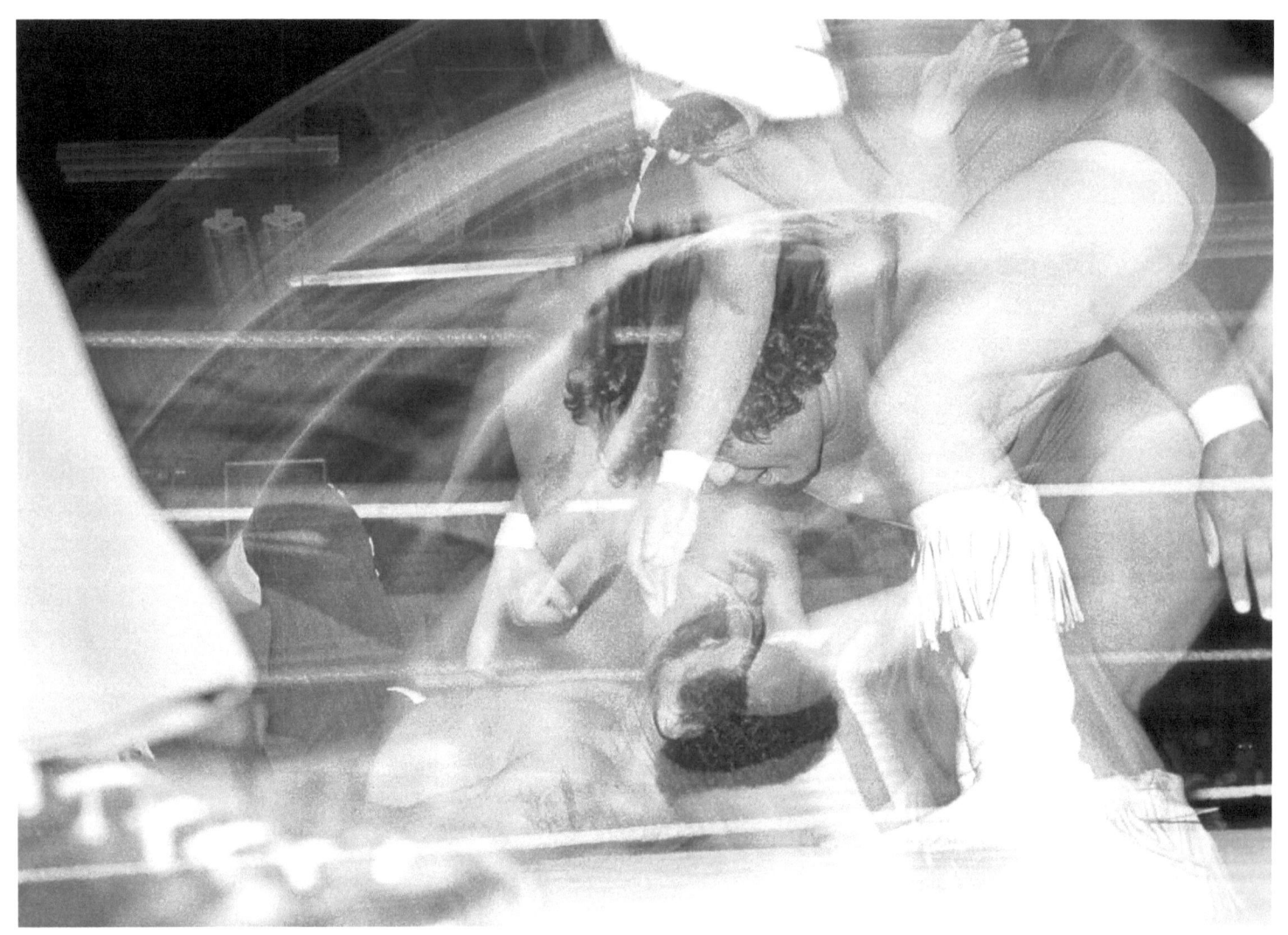

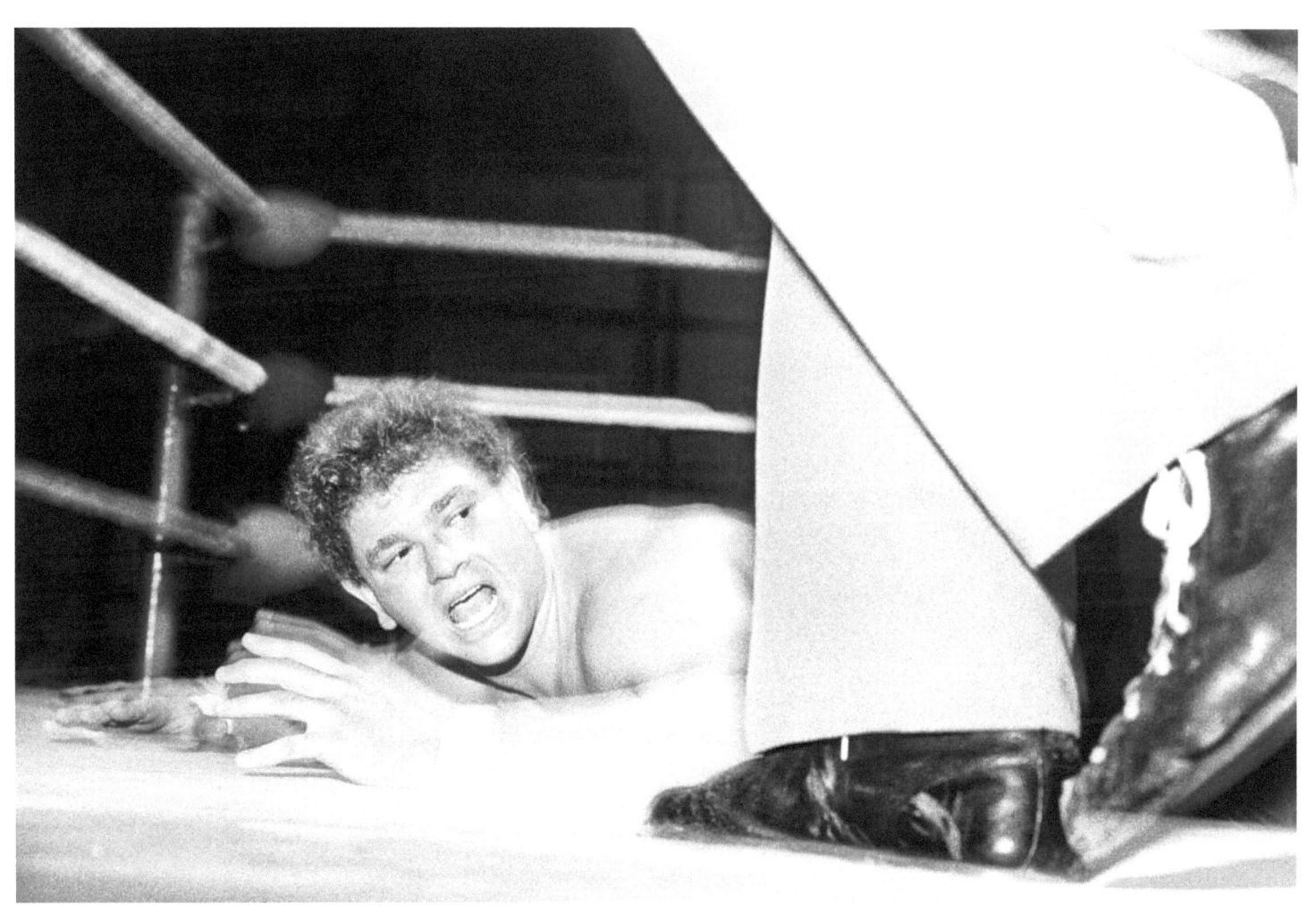

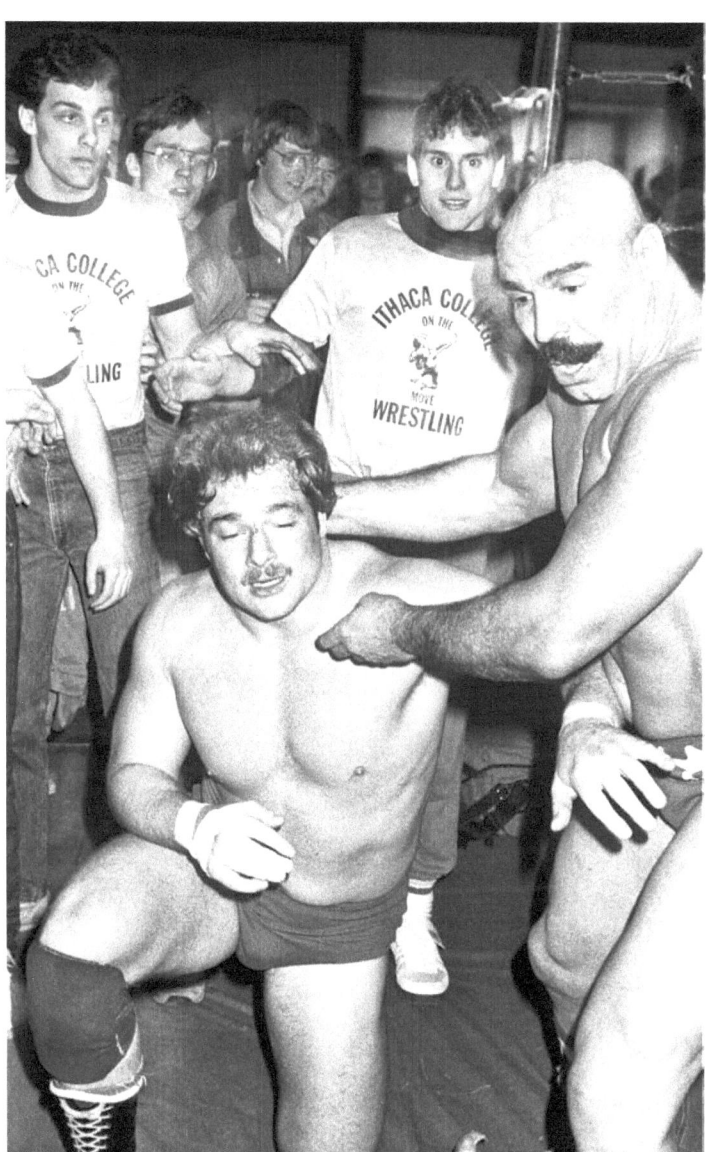

Iron Sheik (Hossein Khosrow Ali Vaziri), 1984

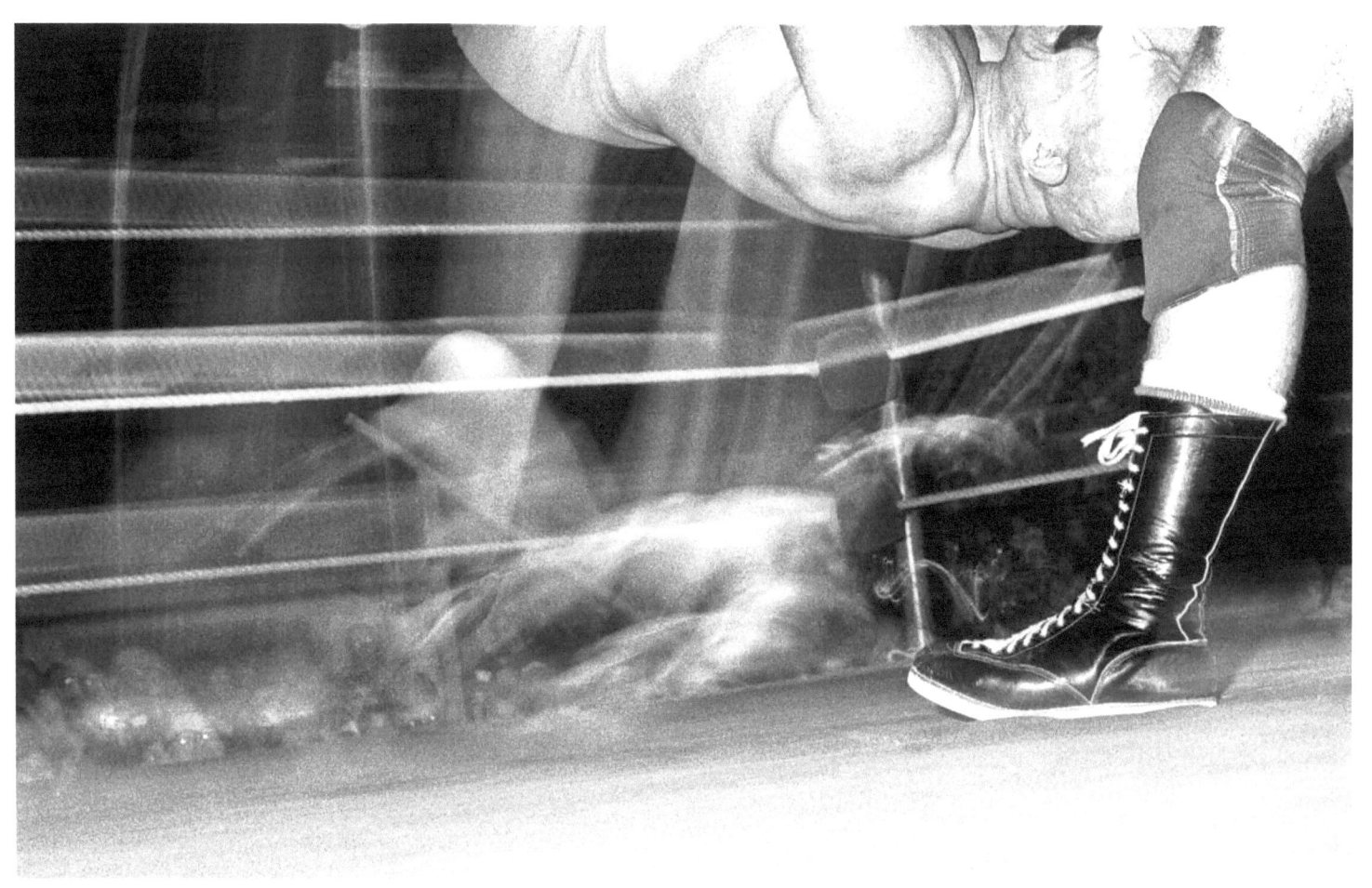

Ivan Putski vs. Sgt. Slaughter (Jim Duggan), 1984

Hulk Hogan (left) early in his career as a heel, 1980

Andre the Giant, in 1984.

Hulk Hogan would later defeat Andre for the championship in 1987.

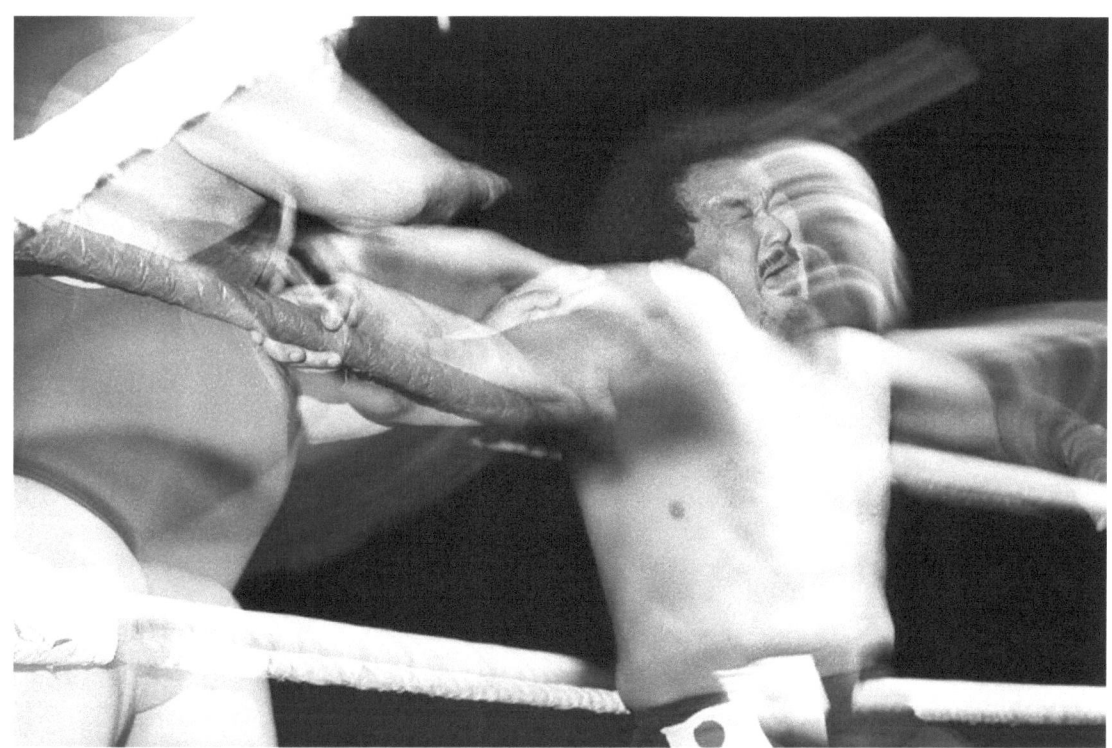

Andre the Giant teamed with Tony Atlas and Rocky Johnson (father of "The Rock" Dwayne Johnson) vs. Mr. Fuji and two others in a tag team match, 1984.

Andre the Giant's favorite move was to sit or lay on top of his opponents until they submitted. This match ends as Andre has stacked up all three wrestlers and with the help of Atlas and Johnson squishes them into submission.

www.ingramcontent.com/pod-product-compliance
Lightning Source LLC
Chambersburg PA
CBHW040905020526
44114CB00037B/61